HOUSE
MATES
a survival guide

Crombie Jardine
Publishing Limited
Office 2
3 Edgar Buildings
George Street
Bath
BA1 2FJ

www.crombiejardine.com

This edition was first published by
Crombie Jardine Publishing Limited in 2007

ISBN 978-1-906051-08-2

Written by Jessica Barrah

Illustrations and cover design by Jessica Barrah

Typesetting by Ben Ottridge

Printed and bound in Great Britain by
William Clowes Ltd, Beccles, Suffolk

DEDICATION

Dedicated to Andy Graney
— Wonky Beak frontman and
housemate. Talented in so many
ways, but never the greatest at
washing up. Loved, remembered
and missed.

Martha started wondering if she had
chosen the right house to move into

CONTENTS

INTRODUCTION

Hell is other people
Total hell is sharing the same house as them

Perhaps you are thinking, "Hell, other people? Hell no! What could possibly be the problem? We just divide the chores and bills equally between us, and whilst respecting each other's privacy, we enjoy spending time together in our communal living space. What could possibly go wrong?"

If this is the case, stop reading now. This book is not for you. Go back to watching the fourth re-run of Friends on E4 today. And keep taking the medication.

If, however, you have ever had a slight problem with a housemate, or have needed Her Majesty's Constabulary to evict them from the house and obtain a restraining order, read on.

I'LL BE THERE FOR YOU

In real life, the obsessive clean-freak Monica would have had a terminal falling out with Rachel a long time ago — probably the second time that some of Rachel's shiny-shiny hair blocked up the plug-hole in the shower.

But don't worry! You too can count on your housemate to be there for you...

❑ there in the kitchen cooking when you want to cook

❑ there in the bathroom when you're dying for a slash

- ❑ there in the living room watching a DVD when your favourite programme is on

- ❑ there having an impromptu party when you've got an exam or an important meeting the next day

WHAT IS A HOUSEMATE?

Housemate [*hówssmàyt*] (plural housemates)
Noun
Definition: somebody sharing a house; somebody who shares a house with one or more other people who are not relatives

The word 'housemate' can also be broken down into two

constituent parts, the first part being 'house' which the dictionary defines as a 'residence, abode or dwelling'. This can also be a flat or maisonette, in which case the correct terminology would be 'flatmates', or 'maisonette-mates'(*).

This part of the concept seems straightforward enough, with only a minimal possibility of confusion

* Not commonly-used terminology

with alternative definitions of house:

a)   building for animals: a building where animals are kept, especially in a zoo e.g. the monkey house or

b)   fast dance music: a style of dance music first developed by adding electronic beats to disco records

It is in the second part of the concept — 'mate' — where more serious problems can arise.

a) The partner of an animal (especially a sexual partner) e.g. "Camels hate leaving their mates"

b) To mate (verb) — To have sexual relations with, to copulate

c) [Brit] Informal term for a friend of the same sex

As we will see, being either friends or sexually involved with a person that you live with can be seriously detrimental to peaceful co-habitation within a place of abode.

WHY NOT JUST LIVE ALONE?

There are quite a few reasons to share your living space with another person. These often include the following:

1. **You are related to them, and you are under 18**

These people are not technically your housemates. They are

members of your family, usually parents and siblings. Enjoy it while you can. You probably don't have to work, pay bills, cook, clean, wash your own clothes or do anything much except mope around the house squeezing your spots, moaning about having no privacy, and how unfair it is that you're not allowed to stay out past 12 a.m. Get over it. You're a teenager. You are lucky to have a family that hasn't thrown you on the streets by now.

2.   You are married to/co-habiting with them

If living with a boyfriend or girlfriend for a few years doesn't make you split up, then by all means, get married. Then you can live together for a few more years, have kids, and then split up. I would venture to suggest that the divorce rate might be quite a lot lower if married couples actually lived next door to each other, with connecting interior doors, rather than sharing just the

19

one house with each other. Then if they did want to get divorced, they could just board up the connecting doors, and carry on as before, with both parties having easy access to the children.

3. You are in prison, and have to share a cell

Unfortunately you will have to embrace this situation. You may find yourself having to embrace your cell-mate too. Watch Porridge whilst on bail, if you think that being incarcerated may be a likelihood, to prepare you for 'doing time'. Study the warm relationship between Ronnie Barker and Kate Beckinsale's dad. Smuggle in as many luxury items/ drugs as you can up your rectum as bartering tools.

4.   You are a monk/nun

Unfortunately, monks and nuns are in it for life. At least if it's an order who have taken a vow of silence, you won't get irritated by your abbey mate's inane chatter about which one they fancy on Hollyoaks, or how Brother Francisco/Sister Perpetua always gets the best bits of meat on a Sunday.

5. **You'd like to, but don't have enough money to rent on your own**

6. **You'd like to, but don't have enough money to pay for your mortgage on your own**

[Solution to 5 and 6: Get a better job. Or rob a bank (although this might land you back in situation number 3).]

7. **You want company**

Having no friends or lovers, you obtain flatmates by putting an advert in the local papers.

Why not follow the lead of spinsters everywhere, and get a cat, or Sky Plus instead? It may save you a lot of stress and bother in the long run. Alternatively, find virtual friends in internet chat rooms. Discontinue the friendship if they turn out to be cannibals looking for people who don't mind being eaten.

8.   You think it would be great fun to share a house or flat with friends

Being both a housemate and an actual mate are not mutually exclusive, but sharing a house is a great way to lose a good friend. You may share interests and the same attitude to life, but when you start sharing a fridge and a bathroom too, problems can all too easily arise. If you value your friendship, move in with a complete stranger instead. Then at least when you fall out you will not have lost anything.

THE IDEAL HOUSEMATE

The Perfect Flatmate?
(and his friends)

The strange thing about house-mates is that no matter how perfect, no matter how amazingly nice your brand spanking new one seems to be when they first arrive, somehow they always turn out to be fatally flawed in some totally unforeseeable way. Unfortunately, unlike a mobile phone, you can't send a defective housemate back to the factory.

The philosopher Plato thought that what we see in the physical world is a dim reflection of the true ideal thing. For example, circular objects are crude approximations to the ideal perfect circle. The 'ideal' housemate does not exist in the real world, but floats above us in some other dimension.

In other words, there's no real point in making a list of qualities for the ideal housemate. Candidates will never measure up in reality to the expectations you have of them, especially as these expectations will vary enormously from person to person.

But hey! Here's a list anyway.

Pointless list of criteria for non-existent-in-real-world 'ideal' housemate

❑ Easy going, but not so relaxed that they are comatose

❑ Clean, but not anally so

❑ Punctual paying bills

❏ Good taste in music (i.e. the same or complementary to yours) with large CD collection

❏ Good taste in films (or the same bad tastes) and large DVD collection

❏ Good sense of humour (or the same rubbish one)

❑ Not so good-looking or cool as to show you up, but not so weird as to frighten other visitors away from your door

Added bonus pointless points

❑ Has a car, and doesn't mind using it to go on the 'supermarket run' or take you out on day trips

❏ Has famous cousin who can get lots of free tickets for VIP parties

❏ Works for a brewery/ travel company, and gets lots of freebies

❏ Has a rich family, with a villa in Spain, so that when/if you become friends you can go and visit

Even if they seem at first to fulfill all the stated criteria, you may soon be wishing that your flatmate/housemate was playing in heavy traffic, due to their annoying habit of leaving parsley everywhere, or stirring their tea over-enthusiastically.

Q: Why did the hedgehog
      cross the road?
A: To avoid having to talk to
      his ex-flatmate.

EXCESS BAGGAGE

Housemates come with all sorts of baggage. Sometimes this can mean a whole lot of stuff you can borrow. It might mean lava lamps and cushions and embarrassing old Athena posters they want to put up. However, unless they want to put a large Nazi flag over the mantelpiece, or have a coffee table made from rhino legs, their material possessions are generally not the problem.

HOUSEMATES - A SURVIVAL GUIDE

Remember - Housemates don't often exist in a vacuum.*

You're not just gaining a housemate, but you're also gaining their network of friends, and more dangerously, lovers. This can be fantastic if you all get along. Not so good if you don't. And sometimes, that irritating boyfriend/girlfriend seems to move in too and all of a sudden you've got an extra housemate without even realising it.

* and often don't seem to believe in the existence of a vacuum cleaner

If you don't even have time to see the friends you already have, let alone make new ones, and prefer not to have unwanted visitors to your house, it might be advisable to get someone who's new in town, and who hasn't got their 'network' set up yet. This avoids the situation where your new housemate and friends take over the living room, leaving you no space to watch Eastenders, even if you could stand them chatting all the way through it.

AVOID FOREIGN STUDENTS (UNLESS YOU ARE ONE)

Foreign students might seem, at first glance, to appear to be a good option, as they generally know nobody in town, and therefore it is harder for them to make friends owing to the language barrier.

However, if your foreign student is on an English course, they'll probably make friends who don't speak English very well either. If they come from different countries, their attempts to converse in English might be amusing to listen to. If they're from the same country they'll be jabbering away in their own language. You can see this as an opportunity to learn something new. Or you could just see it as annoying.

As a general rule, foreign students do not make great flatmates. They'll be no help with paying the council tax bill. They also may not have a British bank account, and won't understand (or will pretend not to understand) the concept of paying bills by direct debit or standing order. Their language skills may be improving daily, but somehow they still won't seem to understand you when you need money for paying those bills, and often disappear back to their own country having run up thousands of pounds on the phone calling home in the middle of the day.

GETTING A NEW HOUSEMATE

I've come about the room...

SATAN
ROCKS

Let's start with the process of getting one. Let's imagine that the last housemate you had spent the last four months of their tenancy holed up in their bedroom playing My Heart Will Go On on repeat, at maximum volume. When they occasionally emerged, dressed in a heavily stained dressing gown, they picked fights with hallway mirrors or passing guests. They made a huge fry up of all your food from the fridge, leaving the kitchen looking as though a Tasmanian devil had gone on a rampage.

43

This time you want to get someone normal. Someone with reasonable levels of social behaviour, hygiene and sanity.

All of your other friends are already settled, and you've already asked them if they know of anyone else looking for a place. No luck.

You will just have to find someone by putting an advert in the local paper, or putting a card in a local shop.

For some reason, health food shops always seem to have the biggest notice boards, full of adverts such as the following:

Vegan, animal loving, lesbian friendly flatshare, looking for open-minded, non-smoking professional F, washing machine, gch, near station, 400 pcm, email treehugger@hotmail.com

Somehow, there never seems to be an equivalent shop with a notice board for adverts such as:

Right-wing, wholly carnivorous (mainly kebabs), homophobic flatshare, ideal for DSS, heavy-smoking M, (or F with big tits, who doesn't mind washing up). Near late opening pub and Ladbrokes. 60 quid a week. No students.

none of them
bleedin' students

Both for those who are searching for a new housemate, and those looking for a room, reading between the lines of this type of advert is essential.

Here is a quick guide to some of the terminology used, to help you in your quest. Term Meaning.

Relaxed
Messy

Chilled out
Constantly smoking weed

Fun loving
Alcoholic

Tolerant
Has an S & M cellar

Vegetarian
No point hiding Pepperami under the sofa

Non-Smoker
see below

Professional
Keep away you student/dole scum. We want someone who will pay bills and gets up during daylight hours

Animal lover
Twenty cats and three dogs. Asthmatics need not apply – there will be animal hair over every surface. Alternatively, they may literally love animals. In the biblical sense

Gay friendly household
Must love Kylie. Own tanning bed and mini gym a bonus

DSS welcomed
No one else in their right mind would want it

Single Room
Broom cupboard

Double Room
Just about squeezed in a double bed, but can't actually close the door

Sunny Double Room
As above, no curtains provided

Garden Flat
Access to three paving stones and a birdbath full of fag ends

Recently decorated
Painted over the damp patch

GCH
Gas Central Heating – boiler in your room, hasn't been serviced since 1983. Or bad spelling of Good Cense of Humour

Near Station/Tube
Half an hour's walk away

Very Near Station/Tube
Basically built on top of railway, trains shake house like earthquake every few minutes

TO SMOKE OR NOT TO SMOKE?

Generally, when a person puts up an advert saying they only want to live with non-smokers, they don't smoke, and don't want to live with someone who does. On the other hand, maybe they just don't want to live with Dot Cotton, but wouldn't mind the occasional fag or puff on a joint.

Six Degrees of Non-Smoking

Why not try this little test to see which kind of non-smoker your prospective housemate is?

Put an ashtray in the room, and spark up. If you are actually a non-smoker, try not to cough. Offer one to your prospective housemate, and see which one of the following responses most closely resembles what they say, and match up to the respective smoking 'types'.

1. No thanks (disgusted look, hand over mouth). I thought you said you were a non-smoker. I could never live in a house with someone who smokes.

2. No thanks. I don't smoke. Unless I'm hammered.

3. Nah... I don't smoke... tobacco... I sometimes have a... you know. Do you... smoke?

4.   I really shouldn't, but...
       [guilty look]. Oh, go on
       then.

5.   No thanks... [longing
       look]. I've given up
       [gnaws nails]. Could I have
       another coffee? Extra
       strong and ten sugars?
       Thanks.

6.   Thanks. Brilliant. I've been
       absolutely gasping for one
       since I came in, but I

thought you'd put non-
smoker on the advert, and
the room looks really nice.

Non-Smoking Types

❑   Never smokes. Violently
     anti smoking

❑   Doesn't usually smoke,
     but doesn't really care
     if people smoke around
     them, occasionally has a
     drag when totally drunk

❏ Occasionally smokes cigarettes. Regularly smokes marijuana

❏ Always smokes in a social situation, and occasionally outside work if it's possible to cadge a fag, but doesn't actually buy them

❑   Gave up two years ago, and ostentatiously went on about how easy it was, and gave everyone a copy of Allen Carr's book. Now secretly smoking again, but won't admit it

❑   May be very moody, and eat everything in the house not nailed down

INTERVIEW TECHNIQUE

The film Shallow Grave shows the 'panel' style interview at its cruel best.

If there are more than one of you already living in the house, sit in a line on the sofa, and perch the hapless potential housemate on a stool, or squirming below you on a bean bag. Aim your anglepoise lamps straight in their faces for maximum discomfort.

Have a long list of questions written out and attached to a clipboard.

Some questions will be relevant to house sharing, e.g. "On a scale of one to ten, how messy are you?". Some will be drawn from the Purity Test – the one that asks if you've ever had sex with an animal whilst on drugs. Others will be random surreal questions such as "Would you prefer to eat a sheep's eyeball or a monkey's brains?" Nod seriously and make approving or disapproving noises at their responses.

This style of interviewing potential housemates is best if the flat or house is so gorgeous that everyone who sees it will choose to disregard the obvious problems of living with such obnoxious housemates.

If this is not the case, it's better to just be as friendly as possible to their faces, then slag them off as soon as they leave.

If you are the Interviewee

You'll probably gauge the general 'feel' of the household by the furnishing and general tidiness of the house and the 'vibe' of the people there — but they may have tidied up just for your visit, and the psycho housemate with

the tattooed face may have been
banished for the night.

Ask a lot of questions. Some
sensible ones might be:

❑   How much is the council
       tax?

❑   How much are the other
       bills?

❑   Is there anyone here who
       works nights?

❏ Are any of you students or do you all work?

❏ Do you cook together?

❏ Do you socialize together?

However, you might want to avoid these ones:

❏ Are there any other girls living here? Are they fitter than you? Are they single?

❑ My ex-housemates were nightmares. They were always going on about tidying up, and cleaning and shit. You're not like that are you?

❑ Yeah, I've been a heroin addict for about four years now. Actually, do you mind if I cook up?

❑   Can I move in
immediately? I've
got nowhere else to go. I
burnt down the last house
I was living in. But I'm
pretty much over my
pyromania now.

LIVING TOGETHER IN PERFECT HARMONY

Ebony and Ivory may have lived together in perfect harmony in Stevie Wonder's song. But they were just side by side on his piano keyboard. It makes me wonder, Mr. Wonder, if you've ever had to share a house? I hate to say it, but if you could have actually seen the mess my ex-flatmate left the bathroom in, then you might be singing a very different tune.

The main problems are usually based around:

❏   Keeping the house clean

❏   Dividing the household bills

❏   Sharing the kitchen, and shared communal food items

❑ Sharing bathrooms —
timings of when in use,
hot water and
cleanliness issues

❑ Disturbance — when
housemates stay up late
or get up early on a
regular basis

❑ Noisiness — especially
playing music

The Young Ones

Special mention needs to be made of the potentially extreme grime of the 'Student' house. You don't actually have to study to live in filth. A good example of this is the shared house in the film Withnail and I.

When you're a teenager, the thought of sharing a house or a flat seems like a dream existence. You can do what you want, when you want, eat and sleep when you want, and best of all, you get to share it with friends.

But after you've got over the excitement of people not caring if you don't change your underwear or bed linen, stay up all night shagging and eating cold curry in bed, you may start to change your mind. Little things might start to bother you. Little things, for example, like mushrooms growing in the living room.

The squalor of the student house could be put down to poverty — no money to buy cleaning products — though somehow there's always enough cash to buy beer. It could be that you are all so involved with studying around the clock that the idea of cleaning is not possible to squeeze in to your overloaded mind. More likely you feel that there's no point in cleaning up — it will all get dirty again soon, and no one else in the house ever bothers.

Something simple like making a cup of tea can become hugely complicated. Usually it goes like this:

1.   Boil kettle
2.   Put teabag in mug
3.   Pour on hot water
4.   Add milk, maybe sugar
5.   Remove tea bag
6.   Stir
7.   Drink

Not so in the student house...

The Thirty Step Brew

1. Find knife
2. Scrape hardened mould off a cup
3. Go to the shop as there is no washing up liquid
4. Come back and wash cup with fingers — there is no cloth or scrubber, but you can't be bothered to go back to shop

5.   Struggle to get the kettle
     under the tap — sink full
     up of dirty plates
6.   Fill the kettle bit by bit
     with the cup you just
     washed
7.   Boil the kettle
8.   Realize that you have no
     tea bags
9.   Hunt around other
     people's cupboards. Find
     stray tea bag
10. Pour on hot water. Notice
     strange odour. Ignore

11. Use last dregs of milk. Realize you have no sugar

12. Hunt around cupboards for sugar. Add sugar. Stir

13. Drink

14. Spit out. Realize strange odour was peppermint tea. Throw away

15. Hunt around for another teabag. Find teabag. Sniff

16. Boil kettle again

17. Realize you just used the last bit of milk on the peppermint tea

18. Go to the shops to buy more teabags and milk

19. The radio and light goes off as you walk in the door. You have not paid your electricity bill, and been cut off

20. Decide to boil water in a saucepan on the hob

21. Wash out a dirty pan, as no clean ones around. Again, you have forgotten to buy brillo pads etc, so clean out with fingers

22. Fill up the saucepan with the same difficulty as the kettle

23. Press ignite on the gas stove. Nothing happens

24. Look around for a lighter, but cannot find one

25. Search for some matches

26. Find a box of matches but they are all used up

27. Find a small book of them propping up the wobbly table. A vase falls off the table and smashes as you pull the matches out

28. Struggle to light the matches, and burn your finger. Matches all go out before you reach stove

29. Finally light one triumphantly, but the stove still doesn't work. The gas has also been cut off

30. Go to a nearby café, and have a cup of tea there

It may be at this point that you crack, and decide that something needs to be done.

There needs to be some organization in this house. Housemates should get together and work as a team...

THE ROTA

You may think at this stage
It's a little too late
To say that some people
Aren't pulling their weight
That I've noticed some people
Aren't doing their quota
Of chores, so I wrote out this
cleaning rota

We each have to tick off our
names on the list
I'll be fining those people whose
turn has been missed
We must face the fact
That we all have a duty
To make this abode a vision of
beauty
And you can stop smirking
I can't fathom why
You all seem so happy to live in a sty
You may think it's funny
But I warn you, I'm not
Paying this much rent
When it feels like a squat

THE ROTA

I know that there's only two
weeks left of term
But that's no excuse, I need to be
firm
We must take more pride
We all need to pitch in
Fungus has grown on the floor of
our kitchen
It's so unsanitary, so unsavoury
There's a drowned dead mouse
in some rancid gravy
There's a sandwich behind the
radiator
We need to act now, not leave it
till later

To clean up our act is essential
because it
Affects everyone if we lose our
deposit

In theory it sounds like a good
idea. Each person should have a
task. Many hands make light work.
Divide and conquer...

However, it seems that more
time and effort is spent actually
drawing up the rota than doing
any of the cleaning outlined on it.

It's like those timetables you make for revising for exams.

You draw it out with pencil. You draw it out again in pen, coded in different colours. You stick it up on the wall, and then completely ignore it.

Even if people actually do the tasks on the rota, it may not be on the designated day. Or the standard of the cleaning may be questioned, even if the task is done. If another housemate questions the way you scrub the toilet bowl, you may be inclined to stick their head down it, so that they can take a closer look at the way you used a toothbrush to clean around the rim.

If you wash up and no one sees you, did you really wash up?

Wash up everything at all times, just after you've eaten for the first few weeks. Never wash up when there is no one to see you. Unless someone else has very recently washed up, and you just wash up one cup in a sinkful of suds. You can then place the mug on the draining board with a sigh as others walk in, saying, "God, I'm glad that's over with. I just couldn't stand looking at it anymore."

Then relax as they all get self-righteous about how Pete/Kevin/Penny (see The Scapegoat) should have washed up their own stuff, as it was mostly theirs anyway. Then

you can all nod, each one knowing
that you know they know some of
it was their stuff too.

What? I wiped
the surfaces
only four days ago!

The Scapegoat

Every house has someone who gets blamed for everything. They don't necessarily have to be blamed to their face. It is usually someone a bit shambolic, who has occasionally set a piece of toast on fire. In this way the equilibrium of the house is maintained, with a general feeling that, if it weren't for this person, the house would be spotless, and the fridge fully stocked. It is only when this person moves out and the cleanliness of the house in fact rapidly deteriorates, that you find out that the scapegoat had been a paragon of domestic virtue.

Milk monitor

There is nothing so annoying in the whole world as making a cup of tea, and then realizing that there is no milk. Especially if you bought a litre of the stuff yesterday. And especially if the empty carton has been put back in the fridge. If you live with a lot of other people, you start keeping an eye out for housemates who regularly have cereal every day, like to make vats of custard, hot chocolates, or drink pints of it.

It can be helpful to live with someone who is either vegan, lactose intolerant, or drinks their tea black. Except then you've got no one to blame when you run out of milk, and then you can't steal theirs.

Bread, cheese or egg stealing is annoying too, although you never quite get so emotionally attached to the idea of having a piece of toast as you do a cup of tea or coffee.

It is a rare flatmate who actually steals proper food, things like steak, which you would obviously notice. Confront them about this out and out thievery. Unless they are grasping a knuckleduster at the time.

You could get uber-anal about it and draw lines on milk cartons or in margarine tubs to monitor the levels. But this won't stop a desperate housemate, especially if they are too hungover to stagger to the shops. They'll always intend to replace it. But they won't. Or not until you've also bought some more in any case.

HOW BIG BROTHER CAN WORK FOR YOU

Unless you're a shallow, brain dead, perma-tanned exhibitionist, with hopes of becoming a TV presenter, you are hardly likely to want real life to be like Big Brother. However, there is one element of the show that would be useful. What you could do is rig up some sort of CCTV in the fridge, to make sure of the culprit before you go accusing innocent people.

Other things you can steal from Big Brother:

Try and get rid of unwanted flatmates by gathering them all in the living room on a Friday night, then play a tape saying "X.... you have been evicted from the Big Brother house. You have one minute to say your goodbyes."

It may just work if they're drunk enough.

The Diary Room — It's good to get things off your chest. Sit on the toilet, talk to the mirror, and imagine there's a film crew behind it.

HELLO KITTY

A kitty is used to pay for communal items such as toilet paper, milk, tea, bread, sugar, cleaning fluids, washing up liquid.*

* This is actually the name of the 'fund' or collection contributed to by all housemates. Please note cats are not legal tender, and will not be accepted in most supermarkets and general stores in exchange for goods.

Rarely has a small feline been such a catalyst for arguments.

You can start off including other items that are 'staples' such as butter, cooking oil, cheese, eggs, but somehow people will do anything to deny that they use these things, or have issues about the type and quality of the items you communally buy.

For example, the oil. Should it be cheap and cheerful vegetable oil of a supermarket brand variety? Or olive oil, which is better for you, apparently, but more expensive.

Should the eggs be free-range? Organic? Reared in a cage so small they've pecked off their own heads?

Bread — "I don't want to contribute as I'm on a no carb diet." "I'm wheat intolerant, so don't think I should pay for bread."

Butter — "I only use it on toast, and usually eat cereal."

Sugar — "I don't need it. I'm sweet enough. "

Toilet paper — It would be hard to say that you don't actually use it, but you may suspect that some people have a larger backside or eat more curries, or use it to wipe off makeup or cry more.

In the end the only things that you'll get to put as communal purchases are washing up liquid and cleaning items. There may be fights over the smell or the eco-friendliness of it, but remember not to say, "Well, I don't think I should contribute to the washing up liquid/bleach/cleaning fluid/ as I never use it."

BILLS

Money is the root of all evil. Not necessarily having it, but not having it. Or one person having it and the other not... Basically if you are sharing a house, you are not wealthy enough to buy your own, so you'll probably be fairly skint. If you are the sort of person who is trying to save energy and water by not bathing, or by wearing three jumpers and sitting by the light of a candle, there will always be someone in the house who leaves all the lights on, cranks up the heating in September, and takes long hot baths twice a day. There is not really much you can do about this.

RING MY BELL

And that's not mine either. I think I might have made that local call on the 20th September. I don't think it's fair if we divide it up equally. Isn't that your boyfriend's mobile number? I literally have not touched that phone for months. I just use my mobile. Maybe we should get incoming calls only. No. I didn't call that number. A sexline in Malaysia? Of course not.

CUM ON FEEL THE NOIZE

Remember how your parents would tell you to turn your music down? Living the house-share lifestyle, you are all supposed to be adults and equals, with respect for each other's space. This includes the aural space — don't impose your music on other people. The thing is, it is obvious when your music of choice is heavy metal or banging techno that people might complain, but be aware that even Dido or Enya can bring on feelings of intense irritation, even at relatively low volumes.

HOUSEMATING

It is definitely not a good idea to sleep with one of your new housemates in the first week, even if 'that fit bloke' was one of the reasons you were so keen on moving in. When going out for a 'getting-to-know-you drink', don't 'get to know them' in the biblical sense. It will be weird for the other housemates. And you are living together before you even know each other properly.

Things can quickly get so intense that you may have split up by the next week, and you still have to live there for the rest of your contract.

And mating with one of the friends of your housemates can also turn out badly. If it goes wrong you may have to hide in your room every time they come round to visit.

But even if you avoid physical contact, depending on the thickness of the walls, you may not be able to totally avoid all aspects of your housemates' sex lives.

Somehow, your parents having sex is the worst sound in the world. You know that they must have done it sometime, to have produced you, but there's no need to carry on doing it after it has produced the desired effect.

However, the second worst sound may be your housemate going at it all night whilst you are lying in bed trying to read. Potential scenarios and sounds include:

❏   Porno noises — they're just showing off. Or actually watching a porno with the volume up a bit too high

❑ The agony and the ecstasy — frightening noises, sounding like they are in pain. You wonder whether you should call 999

❑ The beast — animalistic grunting, huffing and puffing

❑ Minnie Mouse — strange squeaks and giggles

❑ Thomas the Tank Engine — bed banging in a rhythmic manner, speeding up as the train goes into the tunnel and reaches its final destination

HOUSEMATES CAN BE GREAT!

I hope that all this hasn't put you off sharing houses. After all, it's generally better than living on your own in a tiny bedsit or freezing caravan!

Above all, it's important to choose the right sort of house share for your own character. One man's meat is another man's veggie burger. Or something.

Here's a short quiz to help you spot some of the types of houses you might encounter. Try to match the house with their ideal housemate.

Housey Housey Quiz

A. *Party Hearty*
Mounds of salt on the carpet, as someone read on the internet that it's good for red wine stains, but has never got around to hoovering them up. Fag burns and more stains on the sofa — someone

116

threw up on the 'throw' put over to hide the original stains. Mysterious marks up the wall, and glass marks on CDs that have been used as coasters in a mistaken attempt to avoid ruining the table, which was already ruined anyway. Well stocked with paracetamol, Coca Cola and various half empty bottles of spirits.

B. *Backpackers*

The house was originally rented in 1994 by someone nobody in the house actually knows, but since then, successive waves of Aussies, Kiwis, South Africans and occasional Israelis have been through. There are actually four bedrooms, but there are sixteen people in total living there, which really brings the rent down.

C. Ikea Shrine

Chloe's mum and dad have given her the deposit to buy a two bedroom flat, now she needs a flatmate to share the cost of the mortgage, and for company. She's looking for a nice, clean, non-smoking girl to watch romantic comedies with. Her main worry is about damaging the white sofa she got in Ikea.

D. Boys-Toys Bachelor Pad

Shelf full of Lord of the Rings books and DVDs, an old life-sized cut out of Buffy, Star Wars figurines, music magazines… Mike, who works in computers bought the house five years ago, but keeps having to find new flatmates. He's now thirty-three, and all his mates keep moving in with their girlfriends.

IDEAL HOUSEMATE 1

Shane has just arrived from a trip around Europe. His friends told him that there might be a space for him on the living room floor in a flat in Earl's Court, but unfortunately that spot was taken by a surfboard. He is looking for work as a barman, and doesn't have much money for a deposit.

IDEAL HOUSEMATE 2

Neil has just split up with his girlfriend, and is looking for a place to stay. He has sworn off women, and has decided that the next serious relationship he is going to have is with an X box, since his ex-girlfriend banned him from gaming for the past three years.

IDEAL HOUSEMATE 3

Tallulah is a DJ, and generally only sleeps during daylight hours. She's fun loving if a little bit of a slob.

IDEAL HOUSEMATE 4

Imogen has obsessive compulsive disorder, and is always flicking off bits of imaginary fluff. She is tea total, and only likes eating white foods and colourless liquids.

HOUSEMATES CAN BE GREAT!

That's when good housemates become good friends...

APATHY

A CAUSE NOT WORTH FIGHTING FOR

ISBN 978-1-906051-03-7, pb, £2.99

JESSICA BARRAH

HOW TO GET OVER A
BREAK-UP

ISBN 978-1-905102-68-6, pb, £2.99

ISBN 978-1-905102-65-5, pb, £2.99

All Crombie Jardine books are available
from high street bookshops,
Littlehampton Book Services,
www.amazon.co.uk, and Bookpost
(P.O. Box 29, Douglas, Isle of Man,
IM99 1BQ,
email: bookpost@enterprise.net
www.bookpost.co.uk
tel: 01624 677237
p & p free within the UK).

www.crombiejardine.com